DOG WA

WALKS WITH YOUR DOG IN CORNWALL

SUE BRADBURY

WALK 01

ROCK TO DAYMER BAY

WITH SUPERB VIEWS OF THE CAMEL ESTUARY AND PADSTOW ON THE OPPOSITE SHORE, THE HIGHLY SOUGHT-AFTER VILLAGE OF ROCK IS THE STARTING POINT FOR THIS BEAUTIFUL WALK. POET SIR JOHN BETJEMAN HAD A HOME IN TREBETHERICK, SO IT'S ENTIRELY FITTING THAT THE ROUTE INCLUDES SOME OF THE LANDMARKS HE LOVED - BREA HILL, DAYMER BAY AND PICTURE-PERFECT ST ENODOC CHURCH, WHERE HE'S BURIED.

YOU'LL BEGIN ON A PATH THAT TAKES YOU ACROSS SAND DUNES AND ABOVE A BEACH THAT'S DOG-FRIENDLY ALL YEAR ROUND. WALKING AROUND THE HEADLAND TO SEE THE GOLDEN SANDS OF DAYMER BAY BEACH IS A REAL TREAT, ESPECIALLY WHEN THE TIDE IS LOW. DURING THE SUMMER, THE CAFÉ IN THE CAR PARK THERE PROVIDES SOME WELCOME REFRESHMENT BEFORE SETTING OFF ACROSS THE GOLF COURSE, VISITING THE IMPOSSIBLY LOVELY CHURCH AND ULTIMATELY RE-JOINING THE DUNES TO GET BACK TO ROCK.

 SAT NAV: PL27 6LD

 DISTANCE: 4 miles

 TIME: It takes about two hours, with a stop at the church – longer if you detour to either the beach or café.

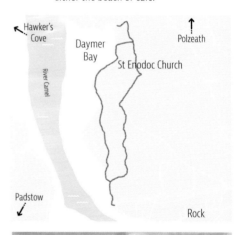

THE ROUTE

Drive through Rock to get to the quarry car park (PL27 6LD). Walk through the gap near the toilets and bear right on the footpath. When you get to a fork, keep left above the beach in the direction of Brea Hill. At the bottom, carry straight on over the lower

2

you back to the dunes and the track back to the car park.

DID YOU KNOW ?

slopes. The track will run parallel with the shoreline until it descends to the sand at Daymer Bay. Cross the little footbridge and follow the sign to the church which takes you to the golf course perimeter.

To see some of the beautiful properties in Trebetherick and get a drink or snack during the tourism season, turn left away from the golf course and towards the houses. Follow the footpath until you reach the road and turn left. The café is on your right, just past the car park entrance.

Re-trace your footsteps afterwards to the golf course and, watching out for balls, cross towards St Enodoc Church. The gate is on the far side of the perimeter hedge, with Sir John Betjeman's grave immediately to your right as you walk in.

When you leave, turn right out of the gate and drop back down to the footpath that skirts the edge of the golf course. Go over the footbridge that you come to and continue along the tarmac eventually reaching a white stone marker on your right, with an arrow on the ground pointing towards the beach. Follow that path – again watching out for golf balls when you walk along the course. The marked route will eventually take

• Originally a thriving fishing village, Rock is now a popular sailing and water sports centre. Its name comes from the quarry, now the car park, that was once used for extracting the stone needed as ballast for the cargo ships sailing out of Padstow harbour.

• There are Bronze Age burial mounds at the top of Brea Hill.

• St Enodoc originates from the twelfth century and, since then, has been buried by sand for long periods of time. Legend has it that one vicar had to lead his parishioners through a hole in the roof to hold a service. Whether or not that's true, the church was dug out from the dunes during the nineteenth century and completely restored. There was even a new bell for the tower – claimed from the wreck of an Italian ship that foundered at the mouth of the Camel Estuary.

• Another site worth seeing is the Jesus Well, not far from the church. Said to be where Enodoc lived and baptised his converts, its name derives from the legend that Jesus Christ visited the place whilst still in his teens. It is said he was with his great-uncle, Phoenician tin merchant Joseph of Arimethea, and that their journey began at Looe, where they landed, and continued to Glastonbury. To see the well, carry along the tarmac drive after the footbridge on the golf course. This will bring you to a small path that takes you to the shrine (grid reference: SW937764).

WHAT'S NEARBY?

Polzeath (PL27 6SP) is the next village on towards the headland from Trebetherick. Hugely popular with visitors, it has a very good surfing beach (dogs are banned during the summer months) and a selection of shops, cafés, pubs and restaurants.

Port Isaac (car park: PL29 3SG) is a delightfully quaint traditional Cornish village that has recently found fame as the location for much of the Doc Martin TV series. Steep, narrow streets lead down to a sheltered quayside and dog-friendly beach, with some lovely restaurants, shops and galleries along the way. It's wise to park in one of the clifftop car parks and walk down as access in a vehicle can be very challenging.

Trebetherick (PL27 6EZ) was once home to Sir John Betjeman and is a bolt-hole for modern-day celebrities. Close by, the art-deco-inspired St Moritz Hotel enjoys fabulous views over the mouth of the River Camel and Stepper Point beyond.

LET'S EAT!

The Blue Tomato café is a short stroll away from the car park in Rock. Dog friendly, the upmarket café has a good menu and superb views of the Camel Estuary.

www.bluetomatocafe.co.uk

For light refreshments during the summer, the Daymer Bay Beach Shop is good value as a halfway point pit stop, with a range of take-away or sit-in snacks available.

Daisy's Verdict

Love this walk – plenty of space to run around in the dunes, easy access to the beach for a quick paddle or swim and even though I have to go on my lead for the golf course and church, I always have loads of fun. Definitely in need of a drink and a share of human mum's ice-cream afterwards!

WALK 02

THIS IS A REALLY GOOD WALK IF YOU'VE GOT MORE THAN ONE DOG AS IT CAN BE ALL OFF-LEAD AND THERE'S A MIXTURE OF SAND DUNES, FIELDS, POOLS, SEA AND BEACH TO KEEP ALL CANINE FRIENDS VERY HAPPY INDEED. THE VIEW IS SPECTACULAR FOR US HUMANS TOO. IF THE TIDE IS OUT, YOU CAN WALK MOST OF THE WAY TO PADSTOW ON SAND – OR TAKE THE COAST PATH IF IT ISN'T. FOR THOSE WANTING A SHORTER OUTING, JUST GO AS FAR YOU WISH – THERE ARE PLENTY OF OPTIONS TO CHOOSE FROM.

TREGIRLS BEACH IS DOG-FRIENDLY ALL YEAR ROUND SO, IF IT'S HOT, TAKE A RUG OR CHAIR AND RELAX IN THE SUN. THE SCENERY IS MAGNIFICENT AND THERE'S USUALLY MASSES OF SPACE.

 SAT NAV: PL28 8HR

 DISTANCE: 3 miles

 TIME: Totally dependent on how far you choose to go. It's about two miles to Padstow so allow at least 45 minutes in each direction, moving at a moderate pace.

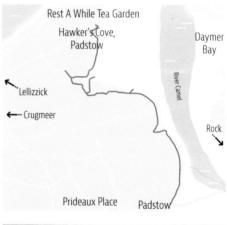

Follow directions for Hawker's Cove. Once you leave the B3276, the road becomes quite narrow and bendy. You'll pass Padstow Farm Shop on your left (well worth a stop). Keep going straight on and the road will eventually bear right, with the magnificent expanse of Lellizzick Cliffs on your left. Carry straight on to the car park on your right, just before Lellizzick farmhouse. If it's closed, you can park on the roadside.

Follow the track towards the beach. There is a stile at the bottom of the car park and the path down is moderately steep. At the bottom you can choose to go left or right – both directions will take you to the dunes. The ground can be very muddy at any time of year and boots will often be needed to wade through pools of water in places. Follow the coastal path all the way to Padstow or do your own thing on the beach or dunes. Coming back, a detour to Hawker's Cove (the hamlet to the left of the beach) is well recommended – especially if you're aiming for some light (or not so light) refreshment at Rest A While Tea Garden.

DID YOU KNOW ?

• Situated on the Camel Estuary, Tregirls Beach, also known as Harbour Cove, stretches more than a mile and a half at low tide – from Hawker's Cove to the north and around Gun Point to the east. Lovely as it is, the sand has also proved perilous. Over 600 ships have been wrecked on its notorious sandbar – Doom Bar - over the centuries. At high tide, it's hidden beneath the waves, fooling sailors into thinking they've made it out of the Atlantic and now have safe passage to Padstow.

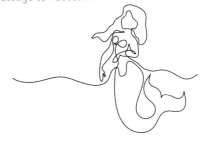

Legend blames the Bar on a mermaid who tried to lure her human lover beneath the waves. When he refused and shot her, she retaliated with a dying curse that resulted in Doom Bar and many drowned men.

• A lifeboat station was built in Hawker's Cove in the 1820s to help those coming to grief in the estuary. It was moved to nearby Trevose Head in the 1960s due to a problem with silting.

• When writing 'Poldark', author Winston Graham used local place names for his characters. One of them was Emma Tregirls – a gypsy who falls in love with a preacher.

Lellizick Cliffs (PL28 8HP) provide the sweeping, coastal scenery for the opening sequence of Poldark as Ross gallops across them. A recent archaeological dig in the area revealed evidence of a settlement during the Romano-British period, with pottery and coins being discovered.

Padstow was originally called Petroc-Stowe, after St Petroc. Recorded as a settlement in the Domesday Book, it is now very popular with tourists and well-known for the businesses that celebrity chef Rick Stein has established there.

Prideaux Place (PL28 8RP) is a beautiful Elizabethan Manor that has been a family home since it was built in 1592. Poldark author Winston Graham was once a regular visitor and the estate has been used as a filming location for the recent TV series. Dogs on leads are welcome in the grounds. www.prideauxplace.co.uk

USEFUL INFO

· THE ONLY BIN FOR DOG WASTE AVAILABLE AT THE TIME OF WRITING WAS IN THE HAMLET OF HAWKER'S COVE. YOU'LL FIND IT IF YOU CONTINUE ALONG THE SOUTH WEST COAST PATH FROM THE BEACH, HEADING TOWARDS THE STEPPER POINT HEADLAND (IN THE OPPOSITE DIRECTION TO PADSTOW).

· THIS ISN'T A SUITABLE WALK FOR WHEELCHAIRS OR PUSHCHAIRS.

· AFTER WET WEATHER, THE AREA BETWEEN THE CAR PARK AND THE DUNES CAN GET VERY BOGGY SO CHOOSE APPROPRIATE FOOTWEAR.

· THERE IS NO PUBLIC TOILET.

· THE NEAREST SHOPS ARE IN PADSTOW – OR STOP AT THE PADSTOW FARM SHOP EN ROUTE.

· THE CAR PARK IS PRIVATELY OWNED AND THERE IS A CHARGE.

· ON A FINE DAY, THE BEACH IS THE PERFECT PLACE FOR A PICNIC.

LET'S EAT!

If the weather is good, it has to be
Rest A While Tea Garden: PL28 8HW. Set in
the back garden of one of the old coastguard
cottages in Hawker's Cove, there's limited
space and no toilets but the view of the
Camel Estuary is amazing and the food –
served from the kitchen window – is award-
winning, homemade and delicious. Cards are
accepted.

www.facebook.com/padstowteagarden

Daisy's Verdict

Loads of sand, dunes to run up and down, interesting smells and water. I can do a good impression of a greyhound running around in mad circles on this beach and no-one seems to mind. Always an exciting adventure.

WALK 03

IDLESS WOODS

CORNWALL MIGHT BE FAMOUS FOR ITS COASTLINE, BUT ITS WOODLAND IS WELL WORTH EXPLORING TOO. IDLESS WOODS, JUST OUTSIDE TRURO, IS ONE SUCH PLACE. ONCE OWNED BY THE BISHOP OF EXETER IN MEDIEVAL TIMES, THE AREA IS NOW LOOKED AFTER BY THE FORESTRY COMMISSION. THERE'S A CAR PARK AND SOME GOOD, ACCESSIBLE PATHS LEADING FROM IT AND, FOR THOSE WHO LOVE A BIT OF HISTORY, THE REMAINS OF AN OLD IRON AGE HILL FORT AT THE SUMMIT. CHOSEN AS A LOCATION FOR ITS LONG-DISTANCE VIEWS AND NOW COVERED BY COPPICED OAK TREES, YOU CAN STILL SEE THE LARGE BANK AND DITCH THAT MARKED ITS PERIMETER.

THERE'S NOTHING LIKE TREES, BIRD SONG AND THE SOUND OF RUNNING WATER FOR INSTILLING A SENSE OF SOLITUDE AND CALM. WITH THIS WALK YOU CAN CHOOSE TO STAY ON THE MAIN TRAILS OR WANDER OFF INTO THE CANOPIED SHADOWS. FOLLOW THE CIRCULAR ROUTE THAT INITIALLY RUNS PARALLEL TO THE STREAM BEFORE GOING UPHILL AND EVENTUALLY WINDING YOUR WAY BACK DOWN. THERE ARE A FEW OTHER WALKERS AND THEIR DOGS ON THE MAIN PATH BUT, IF YOU HEAD OFF INTO THE WOODED AREAS ON EITHER SIDE, THE LIKELIHOOD IS IT WILL BE JUST YOU AND THE WILDLIFE.

 SAT NAV: TR4 9QT

 DISTANCE: 3 miles

 TIME: The walk takes about 1 hour 20 minutes — unless you branch off to visit the fort or explore alternative trails in which case it will probably take longer.

THE ROUTE

You'll find the car park, near Idless village, at TR4 9QT. Go through the wooden barrier at the far end and, when you reach a fork, go right. The track will take you alongside the stream for several kilometres – providing endless fun for dogs that like to paddle or swim.

Look out for a forestry notice on your left that points to the site of the Iron Age fort. If you want the diversion, follow the path beneath conifer trees to reach the bank and ditch of the encampment. Once you've finished exploring there, return to the main track and turn left.

Continue until you get to a point where you can see a road ahead in the distance, then turn left onto a narrower path that goes uphill. At the top, go left again. This will take you all the way back to the first fork – another left and you're back at the car park.

USEFUL INFO

· THE CIRCULAR ROUTE DESCRIBED IS ON AN ESTABLISHED FORESTRY PATH THAT CLIMBS QUITE STEEPLY WHEN LEAVING THE RIVER.

· ROBUST FOOTWEAR IS ADVISABLE - THE WOODLAND CAN GET VERY MUDDY AFTER RAIN.

· THERE ARE NO PUBLIC TOILETS NEARBY.

· YOU'LL FIND DOG WASTE BINS NEAR THE CAR PARK.

· PARKING IS FREE.

DID YOU KNOW ?

TRURO CATHEDRAL

• A mixture of conifer and broadleaved trees, Idless Woods are managed by the Forestry Commission. Look out for red and roe deer, otters and badgers and, in the spring, you'll see the stunning carpet of bluebells.

• The Iron Age fort in the middle of Bishop's Wood is an Historic England scheduled monument. The ancient ramparts and interior are now covered in old oak coppice – identified by the multiple trunks at their base. These would once have been harvested for making charcoal – a common way of managing woodland up to the beginning of the twentieth century. As well as being places that could easily be defended, forts were cultural and commercial centres – somewhere for local farmers to market their livestock, trade goods and socialise with neighbours.

• Idless comes from the Cornish word Edhelys, meaning place of aspen trees.

• The River Allen flows through Idless Valley and on to Truro. Confusingly, another River Allen is a tributary of the River Camel in north Cornwall.

WHAT'S NEARBY?

Truro, with its beautiful neo-Gothic cathedral soaring above the rooftops. A thriving commercial and industrial centre for centuries, Cornwall's only city owes much of its elegant architecture to William Lemon (1697 – 1760), a self-made mining entrepreneur who married a local heiress and went on to become mayor of Truro twice.

LET'S EAT!

The Woodman's Cabin is situated at the entrance to the car park. Open all year round, it has a surprisingly comprehensive range of drinks and hot and cold snacks. Eat one of their delicious pasties, burgers, bacon baps or vegetarian options at one of the picnic tables, whilst watching the stream and world go by. Cards are accepted as well as cash.

Daisy's Verdict

Off my lead from start to finish with plenty of water to dash in and out of, heaps of gooey mud and lots of intriguing smells. Human mum says she didn't hear a peep out of me for several hours afterwards.

WALK 04

CRANTOCK BEACH & THE GANNEL ESTUARY

THERE'S NOTHING QUITE LIKE A BEACH WALK TO BLOW THE COBWEBS AWAY AND THIS ONE IS A BEAUTY. GO AT LOW TIDE IF YOU CAN TO MAKE THE MOST OF THE ACRES OF GOLDEN SAND AT THE MOUTH OF THE GANNEL ESTUARY. THE SEA IS SOMETIMES DANGEROUS BUT THERE ARE PLENTY OF NATURAL POOLS AND COURSES OF WATER FOR YOUR DOG TO SPLASH AROUND IN AND THE VIEWS ARE GLORIOUS.

 SAT NAV: TR8 5RN

 DISTANCE: 3 miles

 TIME: This will depend on how long you spend on the beach but the circular walk up the Gannel to Penpol creek and back should take about an hour at moderate pace.

THE WALK STARTS FROM THE NATIONAL TRUST CAR PARK AND YOU'LL CLIMB OVER DUNES BEFORE DESCENDING TO THE BEACH, TURNING INLAND AND CONTINUING UP RIVER. THE HOUSES AND GARDENS ON THE HEADLAND OPPOSITE ARE SURE TO IMPRESS WITH THEIR FABULOUS OUTLOOK AND STEEP GRADIENTS, WHILST THE CRANTOCK SIDE IS FULL OF NATURAL BEAUTY AND BIRDSONG. HUGGING THE BANK AS IT TURNS RIGHT INTO PEACEFUL PENPOL CREEK, YOUR RETURN JOURNEY TAKES YOU BACK TO WHERE YOU STARTED VIA THE SOUTH WEST COAST PATH.

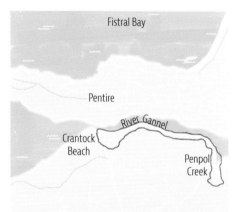

DID YOU KNOW ?

Drive through pretty Crantock village to the National Trust car park (TR8 5RN). Head over the dunes and, if the tide is out, make the most of the space and walk towards the sea. When you've had your fill of watching the crashing waves and hardy surfers, turn back and follow the estuary inland. As it narrows, and the river wends its way towards the bay, you'll probably need to climb a few rocks. There aren't many and they aren't generally precarious but be prepared and watch your footing.

As the Newquay shoreline becomes more populated with houses, you'll see a footbridge enabling walkers from that side to cross. Penpol Creek is on your right. Follow the bank round and, when facing the creek, go to the left where you'll be able to pick up the South West Coast Path. Follow it to the ford, turn right on the road and climb the fairly steep hill. When you reach a stone wall, look out for a signpost immediately to your right that will take you into a field. Keep on the track that runs parallel to the creek and then the beach all the way back to the car park.

• Legend has it that there was once a wealthy city called Langarrow (or Languna) beneath what is now Crantock Beach. To punish its residents for their lazy, decadent way of life, they – and their seven churches - were buried in sand. Archaeological digs in the area have revealed teeth and bones but that is probably more to do with geological evolution than spiritual vengeance.

• The Gannel Estuary is home to a wide variety of flora and fauna – including salt marsh plants, fragrant scurvy grass and vegetation and many species of bird have been recorded there. Historically, the remains of a Bronze Age village have been found at Trethellan Farm and an old packhorse bridge still exists at Trevemper, the estuary's tidal limit.

• At low tide on the west side of the beach you can go into Piper's Hole – a cave that has a flat stone inside it that's been carved with the outline of a woman, a horse and a few lines of verse. Created by local man Joseph Prater, it's thought to have been completed in the early 1900s.

• Penpol Creek was once known as the Port of Truro and you can still see what's left of its quay. Great Spotted Woodpeckers can be heard there in the spring.

Crantock was originally known as Langorroc (translated as the dwelling of monks) and was a thriving little coastal port in the 13th century – long before neighbouring Newquay existed. The village is picture-postcard pretty, with thatched cottages and a circular walled enclosure known as the Round Garden at its centre. Once used for corralling stray cattle, it's a good place for a picnic.

St Carantoc's Church in Crantock is partly Norman and well worth a visit. Grade 1 listed, its many fascinating features include a 12th century font, a medieval stone coffin in the churchyard and the village stocks. The last person to be locked in them was William Linney of West Pentire – described as a smuggler's son and vagabond who had violently robbed a local widow. Somehow he managed to escape via the bell tower and was never seen in Crantock again.

Porth Joke – or Polly Joke (TR8 5SE) as it's known locally – is another nearby beach that allows dogs all year round. Unspoilt, sandy and often much quieter, it's about 15 minutes away from another National Trust car park.

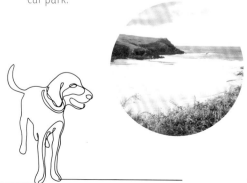

LET'S EAT!

The Old Albion Inn is a charming thatched pub that's around 400 years old. Open all year, it welcomes dogs and serves a good choice of food. Both the main fireplaces have an original pasty oven and the blue stone one in the lounge also conceals the entrance to a smuggler's tunnel that once ran under the village.

www.oldalbioncrantock.com

Daisy's Verdict

Wonderful for running madly around in circles, making new doggy friends and going for a swim or paddle.

No lead required either!

17

WALK 05

DING DONG MINE, WEST CORNWALL

THIS IS ANCIENT, MOORLAND CORNWALL AT ITS BEST. THINK ABANDONED COTTAGES, DRAMATIC CARNS AND PREHISTORIC MONUMENTS WITH MYTHICAL LEGENDS ATTACHED TO THEM. MINERS USED TO TRAMP THE PATH TO DING DONG MINE BUT NOW IT STANDS STARKLY ON THE SKYLINE – A REMINDER OF CORNWALL'S RICH MINERAL HERITAGE AND THE FORTUNES WON AND LOST IN ITS THRALL.

THIS WALK TRULY TAKES YOU BACK IN TIME. WONDER AT THE STONE FORMATION OF THE BRONZE AGE MÊN-AN-TOL, GAZE AT VAST, UNPOPULATED STRETCHES OF WEST CORNWALL AND IMMERSE YOURSELF IN THE SPIRITUAL FEEL OF THE NINE MAIDENS OF BOSKEDNAN STONE CIRCLE. GETTING AS FAR AS THE MINE IS A MUST AND, WHEN THERE, SEARCH FOR THE NOOK AT THE BACK WHERE THERE ALWAYS SEEMS TO BE FRESH FLOWERS. IT'S SAID THAT THE AREA IS HOME TO CORNISH PISKIES AND THERE'S NO DOUBTING THE OTHER-WORLDLY FEEL THAT PERMEATES THE GORSE, HEATHER AND BRACKEN. A GREAT PLACE TO GO FOR OPEN VIEWS, HISTORY, EXERCISE AND CONTEMPLATION – I CAN'T RATE IT HIGHLY ENOUGH.

 SAT NAV: TR20 8NU

 DISTANCE: 3.6 miles

 TIME: The circular route described takes about 2 hours. You can go further if you choose to.

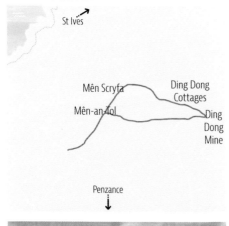

THE ROUTE

Head for the small parking layby that's on the right of the unnamed road between Madron and Morvah (TR20 8NU), not far from Lanyon Quoit and immediately opposite The School House, Bosullow. Go through the gate and onto the footpath.

DID YOU KNOW ?

You'll pass some derelict buildings on your left – keep walking until, on your right, you'll see a stile. Ding Dong Mine (grid reference: SW437348) is unmissable on the horizon. Your route will take you past the Mên-an-Tol so pause a while to look at the arrangement of the stones, two erect, one fallen and one curved with a hole in the middle.

Continue on towards the mine. There are likely to be some boggy patches and you'll climb another stile but keep going in the direction of the mine chimney that's within sight most of the time. Once arrived at Ding Dong, take the wide path on the other side and don't miss the wonderful views of St Michael's Mount Bay to your right. Just before a gate, turn left onto a narrow track and carry on until, eventually, you arrive at the Nine Stones of Boskednan stone circle (grid reference: SW434351).

You're now going back in the direction of the path that brought you from your car. The Mên Scryfa, a standing stone that is 1.7 metres high, is the other side of it in a field and worth a diversion. Return to the parking area or go on walking and exploring if you've still got the energy.

• Richard Trevithick worked as an engineer at Ding Dong Mine in 1797 and it was there that he first developed a high-pressure engine capable of raising ore and refuse from the mine. When the legal representatives of rival engineers threatened to take him to court for infringing their patent, he frightened them off with his own threat of throwing them down the Ding Dong shaft. Four years later, Trevithick's famous passenger-carrying steam locomotive puffed its way into the history books. †

• Eliza Jane Hall was a 17-year-old bal maiden when she died in an horrific accident at Ding Dong Mine. Fooling around during a meal break, she climbed onto a stationary wheel used to haul materials up from underground. Seconds later, her dress became caught in the machinery and she died from her injuries the same day.

• One of the best-known megalithic structures in Britain, the Mên-an-Tol consists of four stones - two upright with the holed stone between them, and a fallen stone at the foot of one of the uprights. According to legend, the very rare holed stone has healing powers and, by following the ritual of climbing backwards through the hole seven times during a full moon, can make a woman fertile.

• The Nine Maidens of Boskednan stone circle was originally thought to have 22 stones but there are now only 11 and not all of them are standing upright. The site is believed to have been used for pagan rituals.

• The Mên Scryfa stone stands 1.7 metres high and is inscribed with the words "Rialobrani Cunovali fili", which means "Rialobranus son of Cunovalus". It isn't clear who Rialobranus was, but he could have been a Cornish king or tribal leader.

WHAT'S NEARBY?

Lanyon Quoit. Three standing stones with a large flat capstone, weighing 13 tons, resting on top of them – hence the Quoit's alternative names Giant's Table or Giant's Tomb. Situated in a field on the right as you approach the parking area for the Ding Dong Mine walk, it's an impressive sight – once you've managed to spot its location from the road.

Madron enjoys stunning views of Mount's Bay. Its church once served the Penzance district and, between the village and the rocky outcrop behind it known as Madron Carn, is a well-known holy well (TR20 8SD) that's reputed to have miraculous healing powers.

Chun Castle (TR20 8PX) is an impressive Iron Age hill fort on the opposite side of the road to the Ding Dong Mine walk. Roughly circular, you can see the remains of several houses, two 3-metre high stone walls and an external ditch. The views are far-reaching.

LET'S EAT!

The Tinners Arms in Zennor was built in 1271 for the masons who built the local church. Stone floors, log fires, low ceilings and a lovely outdoor area make it a perfect place to enjoy good food with your dog in a beautiful coastal setting.

www.tinnersarms.com

Daisy's Verdict

Miles of running, plenty of interesting smells and I even put up a pheasant (didn't catch it though).

WALK 06

TREEN TO PENBERTH CIRCULAR

YOU'LL SEE SOME SPECTACULAR SCENERY ON THIS WALK, INCLUDING FAR-REACHING SEASCAPES FROM THE COASTAL PATH, THE NATURAL WONDER OF LOGAN'S ROCK PERCHED PRECARIOUSLY ABOVE THE SEA AND THE IMPOSSIBLY PERFECT POLDARK-STYLE QUAINTNESS OF PENBERTH COVE.

THE FIRST PART OF THE WALK TAKES YOU THROUGH FIELDS FROM THE PRETTY VILLAGE OF TREEN TO THE RUGGED CLIFFS AND STUNNING VIEWS OF THE SOUTH WEST COAST PATH. DESCENDING TO THE BEACH, THE SCENERY TRANSFORMS ITSELF AGAIN – THIS TIME INTO LUSH VALLEY, WHITE-WASHED COTTAGES, IDYLLIC ROCKY BEACH AND BOATS PULLED ONTO THE SHORE. PENBERTH IS OWNED BY THE NATIONAL TRUST AND DOG-FRIENDLY ALL YEAR ROUND BUT, AS A WORKING FISHING HAMLET, YOU'RE ASKED NOT TO LET YOUR DOG GO ON TO THE SLIPWAY.

WHEN YOU'VE HAD YOUR FILL OF IMAGINING CAPTAIN ROSS POLDARK TAKING A DIP IN THE WATER OR DEMELZA PONDERING THE FUTURE (SOME OF THE LAST SERIES WAS FILMED IN THE COVE), HEAD BACK TO TREEN THROUGH BEAUTIFUL WOODLAND. ALL IN ALL, A WALK OF STRIKING CONTRASTS THAT DELIVERS PLENTY OF MEMORABLE SIGHTS.

 SAT NAV: TR19 6LF

 DISTANCE: 3.3 miles

 TIME: The walk takes about an hour, depending on how long you choose to spend admiring some of its amazing features.

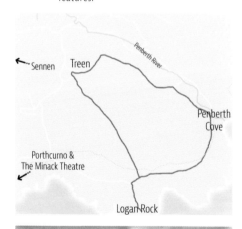

THE ROUTE

Head for the car park in Treen (TR19 6LF). Walk back to the car park entrance and find the footpath to the right hand side of the cottage on your left – there is a sign. Follow the track until you reach a stile, which is marked **'To the Logan Rock'**.

DID YOU KNOW ?

Climb over it and cross the fields towards the sea. Go through the kissing gate at the end and join the coastal path. You're going to turn left to Penberth but, before doing that, walk straight ahead onto the headland to see Logan Rock and the site of what was once an Iron Age fort – Treryn Dinas. There are often ponies roaming free there. To your right, you'll see Porthcurno and The Minack Theatre in the distance.

Turning left, follow the track running parallel to the cliffs, but not too close to their edge, until eventually descending to Penberth. Keeping to the left-hand side of the valley as you face it, pass some stepping stones over the river to your right and continue past the front of a white cottage. When you reach a fork, turn left and go upwards through the woods. Cross the stile at the top, follow the right hedge of the field until you reach another stile. Climb over it and keep following the track back towards the car park where you started.

• Logan Rock weighs around 80 tonnes and is situated on the cliffs overlooking Penvounder and Porthcurno beaches. It's a rocking stone that still rocks – but rocked a lot more before 1824. That was the year a group of British seamen succeeded in disproving the myth that it couldn't be dislodged by pushing it into the sea. The local outcry caused was so great that the Admiralty ordered the rock be replaced at the expense of the lieutenant in charge. Costing £130, the incident is said to have almost bankrupted him.

• Owned by the National Trust which preserves it as a scheduled monument, Treryn Dinas is the largest and most complex example of an Iron Age cliff castle in West Cornwall. You can still see what remains of its ramparts and recent excavations have uncovered pieces of a Bronze Age cremation urn and a Roman coin.

• Penberth has been the setting for a number of recent television series – including Poldark and adaptations of Rosamunde Pilcher novels. Once known for its pilchard fishing, local livings are still made by catching mackerel, crab and lobster. Horticulture also flourishes in the valley, with many exotic species normally seen in South Africa thriving in weather conditions that are unusually mild thanks to the sheltered location.

- THE ROUTE IS INITIALLY FLAT, BECOMING UNDULATING ACROSS THE CLIFF TOP AND DESCENDING FAIRLY STEEPLY TOWARDS THE COVE. THE CLIMB UP THROUGH THE WOODS TOWARDS THE END DEMANDS A BIT OF STAMINA.

- THERE ARE STILES – SOME OF THEM QUITE HIGH.

- THIS WALK ISN'T SUITABLE FOR PUSHCHAIRS OR WHEELCHAIRS.

- YOU WILL BE GOING THROUGH FARMLAND SO MAKE SURE YOUR DOG IS UNDER CONTROL IN CASE OF LIVESTOCK.

- WALKING BOOTS ARE RECOMMENDED.

- THERE ARE TOILETS IN THE CAR PARK AT TREEN, WHICH YOU CAN USE BUT HAVE TO PAY FOR WITH COINS.

- THERE ARE NO DOG WASTE BINS ALONG THE ROUTE.

- THERE IS A PAY MACHINE IN THE CAR PARK AND YOUR TICKET NEEDS TO BE DISPLAYED.

- THERE ARE A FEW SHOPS IN TREEN AND PORTHCURNO.

WHAT'S NEARBY?

Porthcurno (TR19 6JX), where undersea telegraph cables installed 150 years ago revolutionised global communication. The Minack Theatre is just up the hill from the cove and beach – a magical place to watch plays and concerts or simply to visit.

Porthgwarra Beach (TR19 6JW), it's worth driving a little further down the coast towards Land's End to see this beautiful cove. Another Poldark filming location, it boasts a seasonal café that has outdoor seating for you and your dog. Sadly, though, the beach has a dog ban in place during the summer months.

The Merry Maidens of Boleigh (TR19 6BQ) is one of the few 'true' stone circles in Cornwall. Evenly-spaced and carefully shaped, the 19 stones are said to have once been girls who dared to dance on a Sunday. Tregiffian burial mound is also nearby.

PORTHCURNO

LET'S EAT!

Treen Local Produce Café and Shop is next to the car park entrance and is a delightful little place that both you and your dog should enjoy. It only accepts cash though, so make sure you take some. Daisy was particularly impressed with the free dog biscuits the owner brought out and I loved the selection of home-cooked food and delicious Roskilly's ice cream. For more information visit:

www.facebook.com/TreenLocalProduceCafe

Daisy's Verdict

Off-lead most of the way (human mum gets extra cautious near any cliff edges) and a chance to cool off in the river at Penberth. Scampering up the hill through the woods at the end gave me an appetite, so I was very happy when the lady in the café gave me some dog biscuits!

WALK 02
TREGIRLS BEACH,
NEAR PADSTOW

WALK 04
CRANTOCK BEACH
& THE GANNEL ESTUARY

WALK 05
DING DONG MINE

WALK 06
TREEN TO PENBERTH

Porthtowan

St Ives

Re

Camborne

Pendeen

Hayle

St Just

Helstor

Penzance

Sennen

Mousehole

Porthleven

Porthcurno

Mullion

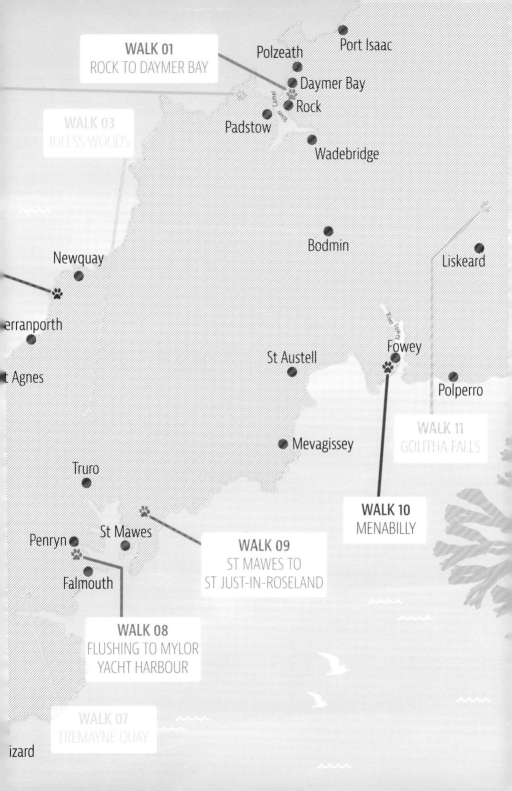

WALK 01
ROCK TO DAYMER BAY

Port Isaac

Polzeath

Daymer Bay

Rock

Padstow

River Camel

Wadebridge

WALK 03
IDLESS WOODS

Bodmin

Liskeard

Newquay

erranporth

t Agnes

St Austell

River Fowey

Fowey

Polperro

WALK 11
GOLITHA FALLS

Mevagissey

Truro

WALK 10
MENABILLY

St Mawes

Penryn

Falmouth

WALK 09
ST MAWES TO
ST JUST-IN-ROSELAND

WALK 08
FLUSHING TO MYLOR
YACHT HARBOUR

WALK 07
TREMAYNE QUAY

izard

WALK 07

TREMAYNE QUAY,
LIZARD PENINSULA

TIMELESS TRANQUILLITY AND MAGICAL VIEWS – THAT'S HOW I'D DESCRIBE THIS BEAUTIFUL WALK ALONG THE BANKS OF THE HELFORD RIVER. WHILST YOUR DOG CAN GO OFF LEAD FROM THE START FINDING INTERESTING SCENTS TO EXPLORE IN THE ANCIENT WOODLAND, YOU CAN ENJOY THE SOUND OF RUNNING WATER, BIRDSONG AND THE RARE OPPORTUNITY OF NOT SEEING A SINGLE HOUSE. IT'S UNLIKELY THAT YOU'LL ENCOUNTER MANY OTHER WALKERS ALONG THE ROUTE AND, WHEN YOU REACH THE QUAY, THE UNBLEMISHED-BY-HUMAN-HABITATION VISTA IS A JOY TO BEHOLD.

OWNED AND MANAGED BY THE NATIONAL TRUST. THE PATH IS GENTLY UNDULATING AND IS A MADE TRACK, WITHOUT STILES OR OTHER OBSTACLES. SPECTACULAR VIEWS AND A SENSE OF PEACE AND QUIET WILL BE WITH YOU AND YOUR DOG ALL THE WAY TO THE END AND BACK. YOU'LL RETURN ALONG THE SAME PATH.

 SAT NAV: TR12 6AD

 DISTANCE: 2.5 miles

 TIME: Approximately 40 minutes each way at a moderate pace.

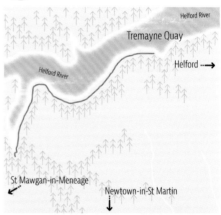

THE ROUTE

This is a well-kept secret! My advice is to head for St Mawgan-in-Meneage (Sat Nav: TR12 6AD) and, still driving, follow signs for Newtown-in-St Martin. The road will meander for about a mile over a couple of old stone bridges and past some idyllic creekside cottages.

Take the unmarked left-hand turn opposite a sign for Mawgan and Helston (the way you've come) and Newtown St Martin's Green (where you'd get to if you carry straight on). It may look as if you're in the back of beyond (you are) but a farm entrance on the left marked **Bunnell** will confirm the route is correct. The road is narrow with some tight bends but there are passing places. As you reach the bottom of a steep hill, you'll see space for about four cars to park (it's also possible to tuck in on the roadside). The gated entrance to Tremayne Woods is on your left.

Follow your dog through this gate and once on the track, keep following it. You'll keep walking on the flat for a while, before the path runs gently downwards to cross the stream. A similarly gradual incline upwards on the opposite side follows the curve of the creek on your left, providing glimpses through the trees of water, some boats and the opposite shore. Once you reach the Helford River, your route bears right alongside it. You'll find a grassy area to your left that's popular for picnics and barbecues but carry on towards your right. Tremayne Quay is at the end of the track. You'll find a little beach there too.
Return the same way.

DID YOU KNOW ?

• Tremayne Woods used to be part of the nearby Trelowarren estate, owned by the Vyvyan family. During the nineteenth century, Sir Richard Vyvyan is said to have fallen for one of Queen Victoria's nieces. To impress her, he invited the Queen to Trelowarren and, in preparation, built Tremayne Quay so she could land there in the royal barge. Sadly, when the big day came the weather was bad and the visit was cancelled. Decades later, King Edward VIII used the quay when briefly meeting the Vyvyans before re-joining Wallis Simpson on his yacht moored offshore and shortly afterwards abdicating.

• The woods, quay and boathouse were gifted to the National Trust in 1978. Comprising an interesting mix of ancient oak coppice once used for the charcoal and tannin trade, the woodlands were also planted with beech, sweet chestnut and holm oak during the Victorian era. The area around the quay is popular with boat enthusiasts, fishermen and campers.

• The Helford River has seven creeks, one of which – Frenchman's Creek – was made famous by Daphne du Maurier's novel of the same name. Looking right towards the mouth of the river, it's the next creek along from Tremayne Quay.

WHAT'S NEARBY?

Mawgan-in-Meneage, like many of the other villages on this part of the Lizard Peninsula, is utterly charming, dating back more than a thousand years. Memorials in the church are dedicated to members of the area's most influential families: Vyvyan, Carminow, Reskymer and Ferrer.

The Halliggye Fogou (pronounced foo-goo) on the Trelowarren Estate is a prehistoric chamber that is one of the largest and best preserved in Cornwall. 'Fougou' means 'cave' in Cornish and this one is roofed and walled in stone with a complex of passages. An English Heritage site, its original purpose is unknown. Entry is free during daylight hours from May to September and dogs on a lead are welcome. Take a torch!

The Helford River was once busy with ships importing rum, tobacco and lace from the continent but is now a haven for leisure sailors. Frenchman's Creek, a little way down river from Tremayne Quay, was made famous by a novel of the same name by Daphne du Maurier. Unspoilt and remote, it's easy to imagine the piracy that might once have gone on there.

The Gweek Seal Sanctuary (TR12 6UG). An excellent attraction where you can find out about the conservation work going on around the Cornish shoreline and, of course, see seals and sea lions benefiting from the keepers' expert care. Dogs on leads are welcome in all areas, apart from the hospital and inside the café.

LET'S EAT!

The Prince of Wales pub in Newtown-in-St Martin (TR12 6DP) welcomes dogs on leads in the bar and gardens. Dating back to the sixteenth century, it's full of character and warmth – helped by a roaring log fire on colder days. The food is very good too.

www.whatpub.com/pubs/COR/331/prince-of-wales-newtown-st-martin

Daisy's Verdict

Off-lead all the way and plenty of scampering space in the woods. Not many other dogs around to worry about either. There's a beach and water to paddle or swim in too.

WALK 08

FLUSHING TO MYLOR YACHT HARBOUR

THIS HAS TO BE ONE OF MY FAVOURITE WALKS – CLOSE TO THE WATER ALL THE WAY, PLENTY OF FIELD SPACE FOR YOUR DOG TO RUN PROPERLY AND NO HIGH CLIFF DROPS TO WORRY ABOUT.

YOU CAN START FROM EITHER DIRECTION, BUT MY PREFERENCE IS TO GO FROM FLUSHING AND STOP FOR REFRESHMENTS IN MYLOR. THE PATH IS EASY TO FOLLOW ALL THE WAY AND MAINLY FLAT, WITH OCCASIONAL STILES. AN ADDED BONUS IS EASY ACCESS TO THE WATER – PARTICULARLY USEFUL WHEN THE GOING IS MUDDY AND YOU NEED TO CLEAN OFF BEFORE GETTING BACK IN THE CAR.

 SAT NAV: TR11 5TZ

 DISTANCE: 4 miles

 TIME: Approximately 45 minutes each way.

THE ROUTE

Sat Nav TR11 5TZ will take you through Flushing towards the Sailing Club. Go past the club on your right, carry straight on and, once up the hill and on the flat, look for a space on the **no through road**. Having parked, follow the pavement through a pedestrian access to the Trefusis Estate and

DID YOU KNOW ?

Kiln Quay. Turning right will take you to a beach bul, for the walk, carry straight on past Flushing and Mylor Gig Club and the back wall of amazing Kiln Quay house. A stile at the end of the wooded area takes you into a field with wonderful views of St Anthony Lighthouse, Carrick Roads and Falmouth on the opposite shore.

The path runs adjacent to the coastline all the way around Trefusis Point and up the estuary towards Mylor Churchtown. When you reach the yacht harbour, walk through the sailing club and keep going (on the path or on the beach) until you see the marina on your right and a couple of cafés and shops to your left.

After a recommended refreshment stop to gaze at the varied assortment of boats moored alongside the pontoons in front of you, return the way you came. You could do a circular route up through the churchyard and via the road but why miss the stunning panorama that the fabulous coastal route provides?

• The house on the other side of the fence as you start your walk is called Kiln Quay. It's a timber-framed manor house that, bizarrely, was originally built in Sussex. In 1919 its owner, wealthy heiress Joan Beech, fell in love with a Cornish sea captain. Unwilling to leave her beautiful home behind when she married him, Kiln Quay was dismantled, shipped to Cornwall and rebuilt. The situation is idyllic – hopefully the marriage was too. † ♛ †

• The walk forms part of the Trefusis Estate. First granted to Richard de Trefusis in the latter part of the thirteenth century, the family still lives in nearby Trefusis House and tenants continue to farm the land. In 1814, there was a dreadful tragedy when a ship called The Queen dragged its anchor and sank on the rocks off Trefusis Point. Full of soldiers and their families returning from the war, 250 men, women and children were drowned. Their deaths are remembered on a gravestone in Mylor churchyard.

• With its popular yacht marina and sailing club, Mylor Churchtown was built around its historic and enchanting church. Dedicated to St Melorus, it has two Norman doorways, a detached bell tower and Cornwall's tallest cross.

• Mylor Yacht Harbour — once the smallest Royal Navy dockyard in the world. Centre for the French Resistance during the Second World War, home to HMS Ganges and the Packet ships and now a sheltered maritime haven. In 2012, it played host to the Paralympic GB sailing team, and Restronguet Sailing Club, which you walk past on the way to the café, was where triple Olympic Gold medallist Ben Ainslie learnt to sail.

WHAT'S NEARBY?

Flushing is an historic, waterside village that is delightfully picturesque. Full of quaint cottages and grander houses that were once home to sea captains and their families, it was founded by Dutch immigrants who built three quays on the reed swamps there in the seventeenth century. Facing Falmouth across the Fal Estuary, it has a vibrant all year-round community, several pubs, a few independent shops and plenty of local character.

Enys Gardens (TR10 9LB) are tranquil, unspoilt and dogs on leads are welcome. The 30-acre estate is especially beautiful in the bluebell season and there are also ponds, different themed garden areas, woodland and a house that is open to the public at weekends. www.enysgardens.org.uk

Penryn (TR10 8LT) is one of Cornwall's oldest market towns. Once a thriving port, it boasts a rich and important history that can be seen in the town's museum, located on the ground floor of the Town Hall.

USEFUL INFO

· THE WALK IS IDEAL FOR FAMILIES, WITH OPPORTUNITIES TO GO ON THE BEACH IN BOTH MYLOR AND FLUSHING.

· THERE ARE BINS FOR DOG WASTE AT THE START OF THE WALK IN FLUSHING AND WHEN YOU REACH MYLOR HARBOUR.

· THERE ARE PUBLIC TOILETS IN MYLOR HARBOUR.

· YOU CAN MAKE THE WALK CIRCULAR BY RETURNING TO FLUSHING VIA THE ROAD, ALTHOUGH THIS MEANS HAVING YOUR DOG ON A LEAD MOST OF THE WAY BACK. NOT A RECOMMENDED OPTION.

· WEAR GOOD WATERPROOF BOOTS AS THE TRACK CAN GET VERY MUDDY.

· THERE MAY BE COWS GRAZING ALONG THE ROUTE.

· YOU WILL NEED TO CLIMB SOME STILES WHICH MAKES THE WALK UNSUITABLE FOR PRAMS AND THOSE WITH IMPAIRED MOBILITY.

· THE TERRAIN IS MORE OR LESS FLAT ALL THE WAY.

· THERE ARE A FEW SMALL SHOPS IN FLUSHING AND SOME GOOD CONVENIENCE STORES IN MYLOR BRIDGE (TR11 5NA).

LET'S EAT!

Café Mylor has indoor and outdoor seating and is very dog-friendly. Serving breakfast, lunch and all-day snacks, it's a very good place to re-energise and watch the maritime world go by. Free dog biscuits are available – although a charity donation is encouraged. Water bowls are provided.

www.cafemylor.com

Daisy's Verdict

Lots of space to run about, interesting smells and places to paddle. Love it!

WALK 09

ST MAWES TO ST JUST-IN-ROSELAND

YOU'LL NEED SEVERAL HOURS FOR THIS CIRCULAR WALK ON THE ROSELAND PENINSULA BUT IT'S WELL WORTH THE EFFORT. ONCE YOU'RE ON THE FOOTPATH, YOUR DOG CAN BE LET OFF THE LEAD, ALTHOUGH YOU WILL NEED TO KEEP AN EYE OUT FOR LIVESTOCK IN CASE ANIMALS ARE GRAZING.

SAT NAV: TR2 5AG

DISTANCE: 5 miles

TIME: Allow at least 2 hours to complete the circuit.

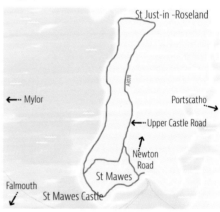

YOU'LL BE WALKING ALONG THE BANKS OF THE ESTUARY ON THE OUTWARD JOURNEY AND RETURNING VIA AN ELEVATED INLAND ROUTE – WITH PANORAMIC VIEWS OF THE FAL ESTUARY VIRTUALLY ALL THE WAY. ST JUST-IN-ROSELAND CHURCH HAS BEEN DESCRIBED AS HAVING 'THE MOST BEAUTIFUL CHURCHYARD IN BRITAIN' AND IT'S NOT HARD TO SEE WHY. YOU'LL HAVE TO PUT YOUR DOG BACK ON A LEAD AS YOU WANDER THROUGH IT, MARVELLING AT THE GARDENS AND THE PICTURE POSTCARD SETTING AS YOU GO.

DURING THE WINTER MONTHS, THE PATH CAN GET VERY MUDDY SO IT'S A GOOD IDEA TO BE PREPARED. IT'S THE PERFECT PLACE FOR GETTING AWAY FROM THE CROWDS, HAVING PLENTY OF EXERCISE AND ENJOYING SOME UNBEATABLE SCENERY.

THE ROUTE

Head for the main car park in St Mawes. From there, turn right and walk through the village towards St Mawes Castle (if you prefer, you can park in the adjacent National Trust car park and start the walk from there). Above the castle, bear off to the left on Castle Drive.

football club and left over the stile into more National Trust land; you'll know you're on the right track if you keep the hedge on your left. Once through the kissing gate, turn left along the road and immediately right at Newton Road. Keep walking downhill towards the quay and car park.

You'll go through a gate with a sign that tells you you're entering National Trust land. Follow the track for about two miles, keeping the estuary on your left and climbing several stiles along the way.

When the path nears Messack Point, you'll pass behind a house and join a drive. Carry on to the right and into a boatyard. Footpath signs will guide you up above the creek, into a woodland and into the churchyard. You may want to pause for a while before taking the right fork near the church tower and passing through the lychgate. Turn left and then right up the steps. Climb steeply up more steps to the right, walk across a drive, climb over a stile and continue walking uphill. When the path turns sharp left and just before reaching the road, cross another stile on the right back onto National Trust land. The path is separated from the A3078 road by a hedge and there are occasional gates, so you may want to keep your dog close or on a lead. Livestock could also be grazing.

When you reach the water tower, join the road and walk along the verge. You can either keep going all the way back into the village via Newton Road or turn right into Upper Castle Road, right again into the

DID YOU KNOW ?

• St Mawes Castle was built during the reign of Henry VIII around 1540 to help defend the area from possible invasion by Catholic forces from France and Spain. Positioned opposite Pendennis Castle across the estuary in Falmouth, it's one of the country's best-preserved coastal artillery fortresses. English Heritage own and look after it and there's an 'oubliette' where prisoners or unruly soldiers were kept underground in the dark as punishment for crimes or misbehaviour. You can take dogs in as long as they're on a lead.

• Legend has it that the distinctive Black Rock that stands proud of the surrounding sea at the entrance to Falmouth Harbour was created from a stone that the local saint threw at a seal who dared to distract him in the middle of a sermon. The stone missed, the seal was unhurt but the iconic rock remains.

• St Just-in-Roseland Church dates from the thirteenth century. Surrounded by a wonderful blend of tree ferns, fan palms, magnolias, camellias, rhododendrons and red cedars, it owes its horticultural beauty to Victorian plantsman John Garland Treseder. Look out for the 55 small granite stones, each engraved with a religious quotation, that line the path from the lychgate to the church.

WHAT'S NEARBY?

St Anthony Head (TR2 5HA) is situated at the tip of the Roseland and owned by the National Trust. There is a lighthouse, beaches, wonderful views, interesting history and more excellent walks. Visit: www.nationaltrust.org.uk/st-anthony-head for more details.

Porthcurnick Beach (TR2 5DU) has plenty of golden sand, rock pools and is dog-friendly all year round. It's also home to the famous Hidden Hut café: www.hiddenhut.co.uk

Poppy Cottage Garden (TR2 5JR) is an acre of horticultural delight. Described as 'the surprise behind the hedge', it opens during the spring and summer and welcomes dogs on leads. There's also a tea room: www.poppycottage.garden

USEFUL INFO

- THE PATH CAN GET VERY MUDDY AFTER RAIN SO WEAR APPROPRIATE FOOTWEAR.

- THIS WALK ISN'T SUITABLE FOR PUSHCHAIRS OR WHEELCHAIRS.

- LIVESTOCK SOMETIMES GRAZE ALONG THE ROUTE SO BE PREPARED TO PUT YOUR DOG ON A LEAD.

- THERE ARE LOTS OF STILES – SOME OF THEM QUITE HIGH.

- YOU'LL FIND A DOG WASTE BIN AT THE START OF THE WALK NEAR THE CASTLE. THERE ARE PUBLIC TOILETS IN THE MAIN ST MAWES CAR PARK.

- THERE ARE SHOPS IN ST MAWES.

- A PASSENGER FERRY RUNS BETWEEN ST MAWES AND FALMOUTH. FOR MORE DETAILS, VISIT: WWW.FALRIVER.CO.UK/GETTING-ABOUT/FERRIES/ST-MAWES-FERRY/TIMETABLE

LET'S EAT!

The Rising Sun pub in St Mawes is open daily from 8.30am for coffees and breakfast and welcomes dogs inside and out. Situated close to the main St Mawes car park, it has good views and excellent food.

www.risingsunstmawes.co.uk

Daisy's Verdict

Had to stay on my lead whilst walking through the village and in the churchyard but apart from that – freedom! Plenty of space to run and chase elusive rabbits.

WALK 10

MENABILLY CIRCULAR WALK

IF YOU'RE A DAPHNE DU MAURIER FAN, THIS WALK IS A MUST. IF YOU'RE NOT – OR YOU'VE NEVER HEARD OF HER – IT'S STILL ONE THAT COMES HIGHLY RECOMMENDED. WHY? BECAUSE YOUR DOG WILL BE OFF THEIR LEAD MOST OF THE TIME, THE SCENERY IS VARIED AND MAGNIFICENT AND, HOWEVER STRESSED YOU'RE FEELING, YOU WILL ALMOST CERTAINLY FEEL BETTER FOR HAVING DONE IT.

THE WALK STARTS JUST OUTSIDE THE PERIMETER OF MENABILLY - THE HIDDEN, MYSTERIOUS ESTATE OWNED FOR CENTURIES BY THE RASHLEIGH FAMILY AND THE INSPIRATION FOR MANDERLEY, THE SETTING FOR AUTHOR DAPHNE DU MAURIER'S MOST FAMOUS NOVEL 'REBECCA'. TAKING YOU TO POLRIDMOUTH COVE, THE BEACH CLOSEST TO MENABILLY WHERE REBECCA'S FICTIONAL BOATHOUSE WOULD HAVE BEEN, THE PATH MOVES UP AND ON TO THE HEADLAND AT THE MOUTH OF THE RIVER FOWEY BEFORE DESCENDING TO READYMONEY COVE. FROM THERE, YOU JOIN THE SAINTS WAY TO BRING YOU BACK CROSS COUNTRY.

 SAT NAV: PL24 2TN

 DISTANCE: 6 miles

 TIME: The walk takes about 2.5 hours – longer if you spend too long on a bench, gazing out to sea.

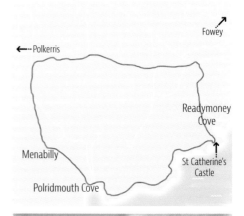

←·· Polkerris
Fowey
Readymoney Cove
Menabilly
St Catherine's Castle
Polridmouth Cove

THE ROUTE

Turn off the A3082 Par to Fowey road towards Polkerris and The Rashleigh Inn. Carry straight on past the entrance to Menabilly on your left and towards the small car park at Menabilly Barton. The car park is on farmland and there's a small honesty box charge of 50p to pay.

When you leave the field, turn right on the road. At the farmhouse, continue through the bollards onto the path. This will descend to Polridmouth Cove (pronounced 'Pridmouth'). Turn left after the gate, following the route along the beach (dog-friendly all year-round), past Polridmouth Cottage (run as a holiday let by the Rashleighs) and up the fairly steep slope beyond. At the top, you'll pass through a gate and turn right into a field. The path skirts the edge before eventually emerging onto a track with hedges on either side. When you see a car park on your right, there will be an option to follow the tarmacked road straight on or turn right on the footpath. Take that right fork, signposted Coombe Haven and Readymoney.

The view from the headland when you reach it is well worth a pause on one of the benches placed there for that purpose. When you've had your fill and your dog is pestering for more exploration, carry on towards the gate leading to the next cove and, in the distance, Fowey. You could take the time to do a momentary diversion right to St Catherine's Castle when the path divides, if not, turn left, carry on along the path and, rather than turning right to descend to the beach, continue uphill and keep going until you reach the road. At the junction, turn immediately left, followed by right, walking past Lankelly Farm and a road sign telling you you're on Prickly Post Lane. After this, turn left onto the Saints Way. Continue walking all the way through the tiny hamlets of Trenant and Tregaminion until you emerge into a farmyard. Carry on following the footpath signs until you reach the Menabilly road a little further on. Turn left, pass the Tregaminion Chapel of Ease, the entrance to Menabilly estate and finally you're back at the car park.

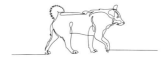

DID YOU KNOW ?

• Daphne du Maurier fell in love with Menabilly when she was living in Fowey. At the time, the estate had fallen into disrepair because the Rashleigh who owned it preferred living in another of his homes near Okehampton. Daphne would walk to the mansion, peer into its windows and dream of living there. She imagined it as Manderley in her novel 'Rebecca', written in 1938, and finally became its mistress when she and her husband leased it in 1943. Having restored the house with the proceeds from her writing, the author and her family lived there for 26 years until a new generation of Rashleighs returned to take up residence. Daphne moved to Kilmarth, a smaller residence nearby, where she died in 1989. Menabilly itself remains a private home.

• Gribbin Head is hard to miss thanks to its tall, distinctive daymark. Built in 1832 and painted red and white, it stands as a beacon for sailors - warning them of Fowey's rocky, narrow harbour entrance. The tower is open every Sunday from July to September for those wanting to climb its 109 steps. To find out more, visit: www.nationaltrust.org.uk/fowey-estuary/features/gribbin-daymark

• Readymoney Cove has a small sandy beach which faces south east. Sadly, you won't find cash growing on trees there – its name derives from the Cornish Porth Mundy, meaning mineral house cove. Daphne du Maurier rented Readymoney Cottage for a few years during the Second World War and wrote Hungry Hill there.

WHAT'S NEARBY?

Fowey, a charming riverside town with pretty, higgledy-piggledy streets, quaint cottages and a fascinating past. The main car park is at the top of the town (PL23 1HA). People started living in the area during Medieval times and piracy, smuggling and intrigue were certainly not uncommon. In 1457, the French attacked the town but, thanks to Dame Elizabeth Treffry who quickly rallied her men in her husband's absence, the foreigners are said to have been repelled with molten lead poured from the top of Place House.

Castledore (PL24 2UA), an Iron Age hill fort, consisting of two ditches around a circular area. Excavated in the 1930s, the remains of 20 round houses were found in its interior. According to Arthurian legend, it was once home to King Mark of Cornwall.

The Saints Way is a 27-mile, coast to coast trail from Padstow to Fowey. Thought to follow the path of early Christians travelling from Ireland and Wales to Brittany or Spain, it passes through Little Petherick, St Breock Downs and Lanivet before joining the Fowey River near Lostwithiel.

GRIBBIN HEAD

USEFUL INFO

• THERE ARE SOME STEEP GRADIENTS, NARROW TRACKS AND GATES.

• THE WALK ISN'T SUITABLE FOR PUSHCHAIRS OR WHEELCHAIRS.

• PARTS OF THE ROUTE CAN GET EXTREMELY MUDDY AFTER RAIN SO CHOOSE APPROPRIATE FOOTWEAR.

• THERE ARE PUBLIC TOILETS IN READYMONEY COVE.

• THERE ARE NO DOG WASTE BINS ALONG THE ROUTE.

• PARKING AT MENABILLY BARTON COSTS 50P – PAYABLE IN A MILK CHURN BESIDE THE FARMHOUSE.

• YOU'LL FIND A GOOD SELECTION OF SHOPS IN FOWEY.

LET'S EAT!

Head for The Rashleigh Inn in Polkerris. Otherwise known as 'The Inn on the Beach', the pub enjoys incredible sea views, a very good menu and welcomes dogs (there's a jar of dog biscuits on the bar). Be aware, though, that the beach itself has a seasonal dog ban from Easter to 1st October.

www.therashleighinnpolkerris.co.uk

Daisy's Verdict

Fantastic! Plenty of exploring, no scary cliff edges for human mum to panic about, lots of running and a bit of paddling. Didn't get all the dreamy sighs about Manderley though...

WALK II

GOLITHA FALLS

THIS IS A BEAUTIFUL WOODLAND WALK IN THE BODMIN MOOR AREA, ROUGHLY MID-WAY BETWEEN THE A30 AND A38 (THOUGH CLOSER TO THE LATTER). POPULAR WITH VISITORS, IT'S NONETHELESS EASY TO FIND YOURSELF TOTALLY ALONE ON ONE OF THE MANY NARROW, SOMETIMES STEEP PATHS THAT LEAD DOWN TO THE BABBLING WATER'S EDGE OR UP INTO THE TREES.

A NATIONAL NATURE RESERVE AND AN OFFICIALLY DESIGNATED SITE OF SPECIAL SCIENTIFIC INTEREST (SSSI) THANKS TO ITS WOODLAND FLORA, THE RIVER DROPS 90-METRES ALONG THE FLOOR OF THE GORGE – RESULTING IN A SERIES OF SPECTACULAR CASCADES AS IT TUMBLES ALONG ON ITS JOURNEY TOWARDS THE SEA IN FOWEY. THE OAK WOODS ON EITHER SIDE HAVE EXISTED FOR AT LEAST A THOUSAND YEARS AND HIGH HUMIDITY, COUPLED WITH ABOVE AVERAGE RAINFALL AND UNPOLLUTED AIR, HAS LED TO RARE, VERY SLOW-GROWING MOSSES, LIVERWORTS AND LICHENS. AN ANCIENT, MAGICAL PLACE THAT WILL GET YOU WONDERING AS WELL AS WALKING.

SAT NAV: PL14 6RU

DISTANCE: 2.5 miles

TIME: Allow about 40 minutes if you just go along the river to the Falls and back – longer if you decide to wander up and down some of the many other paths.

THE ROUTE

You're heading for Draynes Bridge (PL14 6RU), a mile west of St Cleer. There's a fairly large, free car park and two entrances into the wood immediately opposite.

If you take the one on the left, you'll find an information board and map. To make the most of the Golitha Falls experience, I suggest keeping the river to your left and walking alongside as far as possible. This is quite easy at first, but the path does become less wide and more challenging with tree roots and very uneven ground.

The upper end of the cascades and mini falls is marked by a large flat rock by the side of the river. Whilst you could just go back the way you came from here, I suggest heading up the hillside. There are a number of track options – all of which are quite steep. The effort is worthwhile, though, for the different perspective you get looking down on the river and the quiet, tree-canopied calm of the ancient woodland.

At the top of the hill, you'll find a stone wall. Turn right and follow it until it eventually descends back down towards the car park.

• Doniert, one of Cornwall's last kings, is said to have been drowned while either fighting or hunting at Golitha Falls in AD875. King Doniert's Stone was erected nearby (PL14 6EG) in his memory. Preserved by English Heritage, the inscription reads: '"Doniert rogavit pro anima", translated as "Doniert ordered this for his soul".

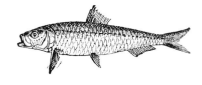

• The source of the River Fowey is close to Brown Willy, Cornwall's highest point. It flows down from there, through Draynes Wood and ultimately on to Fowey, where it meets the sea. Originally a large boulder, known as the Golitha stone (Golitha means obstacle), blocked part of the fast-flowing water and created a waterfall. It was blasted away in the nineteenth century to allow salmon to migrate further upstream. As well as salmon, sea trout, eel and bullhead are among the fish species and there are toads, frogs, otters, dormice, horse-shoe bats and breeding birds like the dipper and grey wagtail. Along the riverbank, a wide range of plants includes lady fern, wild angelica, hemlock water-dropwort, common violet, opposite-leaved saxifrage and navelwort.

• Draynes Wood is recorded in the Domesday Book of 1086.

• One of the underground entrances (known as an adit) to the Wheal Victoria Copper Mine can be found in the woods. Started in 1844, the mine was abandoned two years later, re-opened in 1851 and finally shut for good in 1855. Thousands of pounds had been spent trying to find similar rich lodes to those discovered at nearby Caradon Hill – sadly to no avail.

WHAT'S NEARBY?

Trevethy Quoit (PL14 5JY) is a well-preserved Neolithic 'dolmen' burial chamber. At a height of 2.7 metres, its five standing stones, surmounted by a huge capstone, are very impressive.

The Hurlers (PL14 5LE) is a unique grouping of three stone circles that is managed by English Heritage. Legend has it that the stones are the remains of men who were turned to stone after daring to play hurling on a Sunday.

Minions (PL14 5LF) is the highest village in Cornwall. Developed on a moorland site between 1863 and 1880, it provided a base for those working in the mining, quarrying and railway industries.

LET'S EAT!

Inkie's Smokehouse BBQ is in the Golitha Falls car park. An absolute gem of a café, it's award-winning, very good value and extremely dog-friendly. Daisy enjoyed her first ever 'Doggy Ice-Cream' there and wolfed it down. Make sure you take cash though as Inkie's doesn't accept cards but does do PayPal.

www.inkiessmokehousebbq.com

Daisy's Verdict

Loved the woods and the water – and best of all was my very own doggy ice-cream (Cheddar cheese and sweet potato flavoured). Yum!

47

If you enjoyed 'DOG WALKS' you may also like these...

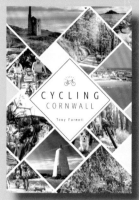

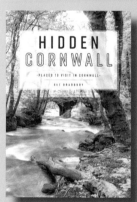

TOR MARK

Published by Tor Mark,
United Downs Industrial Estate,
St Day, Redruth, Cornwall TR16 5HY

www.tormark.co.uk

First published 2018, this reprint 2019

ISBN 978 0 85025 448 8

Printed and bound in Great Britain
by St Austell Printing Company

For information on all titles published by Tor Mark,
please visit www.tormark.co.uk